Unforgettable
INVITATIONS

Melissa Collette Giles

Create Unique Announcements
for Every Occasion

Tips & Techniques to Spark
Your Imagination

come...

C&T PUBLISHING

Text © 2006 Melissa Collette Giles

Artwork © 2006 C&T Publishing, Inc.

Publisher: **Amy Marson**

Editorial Director: **Gailen Runge**

Acquisitions Editor: **Jan Grigsby**

Editor: **Stacy Chamness**

Copyeditor/Proofreader: **Wordfirm Inc.**

Cover Designer: **Kristy K. Zacharias**

Book Designer: **Kerry Graham; Staci Harpole, Cubic Design**

Production Assistant: **Kerry Graham**

Illustrator: **Kiera Lofgreen**

Photography: **C&T Publishing, Inc.,** unless otherwise noted

**Published by C&T Publishing, Inc.,
P.O. Box 1456, Lafayette, CA 94549**

Attention teachers: C&T Publishing, Inc., encourages you to use this book as a text for teaching. Contact us at 800-284-1114 or www.ctpub.com for more information about the C&T Teachers Program.

Library of Congress Cataloging-in-Publication Data

Giles, Melissa Collette

Unforgettable invitations : create unique announcements for every occasion : tips & techniques to spark your imagination / Melissa Collette Giles.

p. cm.

ISBN-13: 978-1-57120-351-9 (paper trade)

ISBN-10: 1-57120-351-6 (paper trade)

1. Invitation cards. 2. Handicraft. I. Title.

TT872.G556 2006

745.594'1—dc22

2005020110

Printed in China

10 9 8 7 6 5 4 3 2 1

Contents

Acknowledgments

I have been blessed to be surrounded by friends and family who have always encouraged me to dream big. I owe a huge thank you to all of you for your love and support, especially to my parents, who have always had confidence in my abilities. I also want to thank the many enthusiastic and professional people at C&T for believing in me and making it possible for me to fulfill this dream. Most of all, thank you to my husband, Greg, for always encouraging and believing in my dreams and for being "Super Dad" while I've been locked away in my art room creating this book.

Introduction

I have been in your shoes before. I've set out to make invitations for a special occasion and have wished for some fresh inspiration. I searched high and low for the perfect guide to give me direction. When I couldn't find it, I decided that I needed to be the author. I hope this book will help simplify the process of creating invitations and inspire you to put together invitations that you are excited to share with your guests.

Unforgettable Invitations *is overflowing with invitation techniques and designs. I have included a variety of ideas for every budget, ability level, and occasion. If you find that one of the invitations fits your specific needs, re-create it exactly. If you are feeling adventurous, apply the techniques, refer to the patterns, and create an invitation tailored to your special needs. As you can see from the invitations that follow, one invitation can provide inspiration for countless variations.*

A handmade invitation can add a personal touch to any special event in your life. So pull up a chair, be inspired, and start creating.

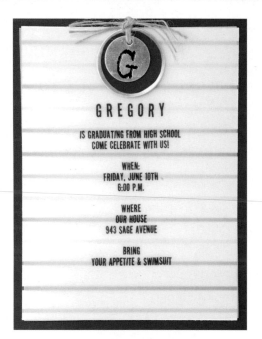

Getting Started

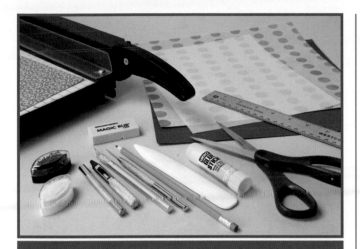

Basic Tools & Supplies

I recommend your local art, scrapbook, or craft store as a great resource for tools and supplies. Some supplies are also available in the art or craft sections of large mass merchants. Many retail outlets sell craft and scrapbook products online. I have listed some of my favorite websites in Supply Sources, pages 57–63.

- Colored cardstock
- Patterned paper
- Vellum
- Paper trimmer
- Scissors
- X-Acto knife
- Metal-edged ruler
- Bone folder
- Awl
- Pencil
- Eraser
- Eyelet punch and setter
- Glue stick
- Glue Dots
- Mono-adhesive
- Fluid chalk ink

Planning

Take the time to plan your invitations and you will prevent a lot of frustration. You will more accurately estimate the amount of supplies needed for your invitations, and you will end up with the result you envisioned. So before you run out to the store, make sure to ask yourself the following questions.

Practical Concerns

- How many invitations do I need to make for this event?

- What is my budget per invitation? (Don't forget to consider the cost of postage, if necessary.)

- How much time do I have to spend on this project?

Creative Concerns

- What shape and size should the finished invitations be? (If you plan on using premade envelopes, I would recommend finding them first to ensure your invitations will fit.) How should the invitations be oriented? (Would they look best vertical or horizontal?)

- What invitation would work well for my occasion and abilities?

- How do I want to embellish my invitations? (Would ribbon, buttons, tags, or another fun item best enhance the invitation?)

- How formal/casual is this event? How can I convey this with the invitation style, paper, fonts, colors, and embellishments I use?

Invitation text

Once you have made these basic decisions about your invitation, you can begin focusing on your invitation text.

First, decide what information would be helpful for your guests to know about the event. In most cases, you'll need to include the date, time, and location. You may also choose to include information regarding "R.S.V.P.ing," parking, gift registries, dress code, driving directions, and any additional information that will help your guests arrive at the right place, at the right time, dressed appropriately, and ready for a good time!

Next, decide how you want this text written on your invitations.

Using a Computer

Your invitation will look more organized if you use a larger or bold font to highlight the guest of honor's name and for words such as **what**, **when**, and **where**.

Take time to find fonts that fit your invitation style. A great font can inexpensively add a lot of personality and style to your announcements.

Because an invitation is usually fairly small, I generally use only one font. When a second font is used, the two fonts should complement each other while being noticeably different.

A great place to purchase font CDs at an economical price is at craft stores. You can also buy fonts online, which is a great option if you want to pick out your fonts individually and use them instantly.

Handwriting

If you are confident in your handwriting, use it on your invitation! Your own writing will add a personal touch. You can save time by writing out one "master invitation" and photocopying that one as many times as necessary.

Refer to pages 46–48 for ideas on enhancing your invitation text.

You Are Invited

Tip

If you prefer not to use your handwriting, consider using rub-on alphabets, rubber stamps, or letter stickers for your invitation text.

Invitation Styles

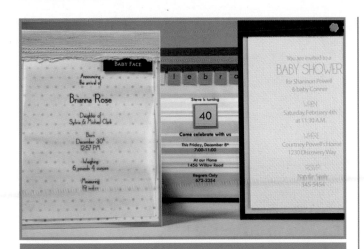

Invitations with a Fold-Over

This is a very versatile technique. It can be simplified or enhanced to fit your time constraints and the occasion. Using this technique, you can put many invitations together relatively quickly and still end up with an impressive result. However, if you have more time, you can embellish this basic invitation in countless ways.

Making a fold-over

1. Print out your invitation. A nice effect is created if you print it out on vellum. Trim the invitation to the size you want it to be. Be sure to leave an extra 1¼″ on the top, which will be covered by the fold-over.

2. Cut a piece of patterned paper the same size as the invitation.

3. Cut a piece of solid cardstock 1½″ longer and ½″ wider than the invitation. This will allow for a ¼″ border around the sides of the invitation.

4. Score and fold over the top edge of the solid cardstock 1¼″ from the top.

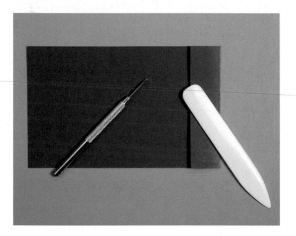

5. Align your invitation layers. The invitation should have ¼″ margins on the left, right, and bottom, and the fold-over should be 1¼″ wide. Adhere the folded-over edge of the invitation with glue.

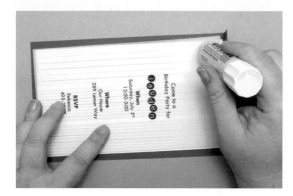

6. Embellish the folded edge.

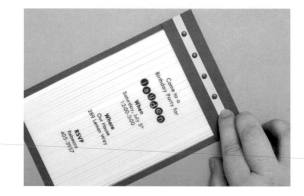

TIP

If you print your invitation onto vellum, be sure to let it dry completely before handling.

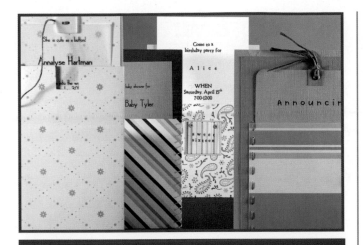

Invitations with a Pocket

Make your invitation more interesting by creating a pocket for it. Throughout the book are many different types of pockets. Once you have created your pocket, have fun embellishing it! Here are instructions for a basic pocket design.

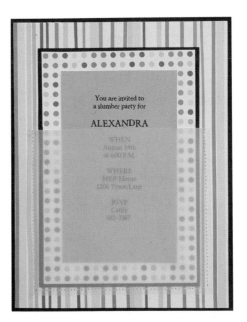

Making a pocket

1. Make the invitation that will go inside the pocket. Determine the material you want the pocket to be made of. Vellum, organza, fabric, or patterned paper can make a great pocket. Choose a material that matches or complements your invitation.

2. Cut the base of the pocket to be 1½″ wider than the width of the invitation and 1¼″ taller than the height of the invitation.

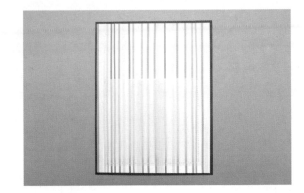

3. Cut the pocket to be ½″ wider than the invitation and ¼″ taller than your desired pocket height to allow a ¼″ border around the sides and bottom of the pocket, where it will be adhered to the pocket base.

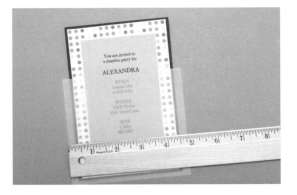

4. Attach the pocket to the base with glue, stitching, eyelets, or some other method of your choice.

Invitations with a Wraparound

A wraparound *is a contemporary way to close an invitation while simultaneously dressing it up. A wraparound is a paper strip about 1˝ wide and long enough to go around the entire invitation and connect to itself. A variety of embellished wraparounds are shown throughout this book. Look for one that inspires you for your invitation.*

Making a wraparound

1. Make your invitation. Cut a paper strip 1˝ in width.

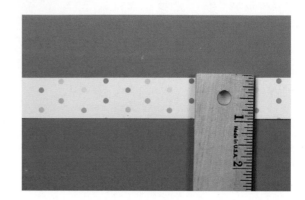

2. Determine the length of the wraparound and cut the paper strip to the correct length. To calculate the length of the wraparound needed, measure the width of your invitation, then double that and add 1˝. For example, a 5˝-wide invitation would need an 11˝-long wraparound strip. Embellish your wraparound.

3. Fold the wraparound strip around the invitation, one side at a time, starting at the front.

4. Draw a line halfway down each end of the wraparound, ¼″ from the edge.

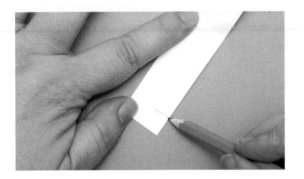

5. Cut a slit on this line.

6. Connect the two ends and secure them in place with Glue Dots.

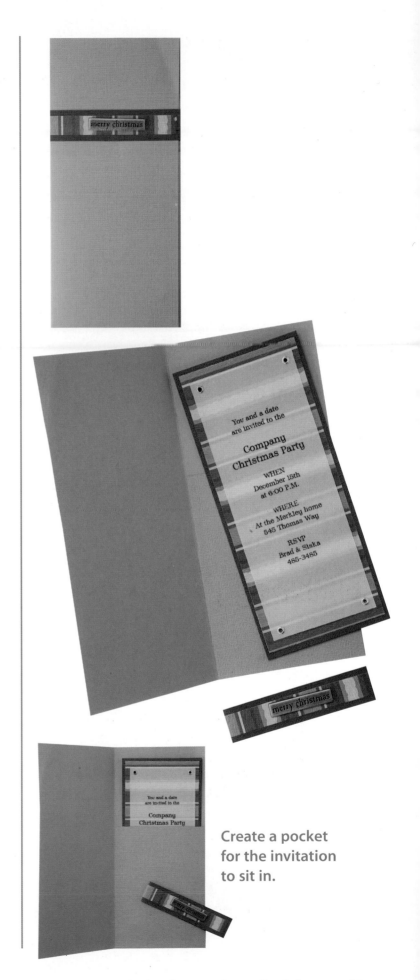

Create a pocket for the invitation to sit in.

This folded envelope is easy to make. See the pattern on the pullout.

Invitations with Creative Folds

It can be a lot of fun to make an invitation with creative folds. All these invitations can be created using 8 ½″ x 11″ or 12″ x 12″ paper, and the patterns can be found on the pullout. Be sure to use paper that is nice looking on both sides, such as cardstock or double-sided patterned paper. Here are a few tips to keep in mind as you put your creatively folded invitation together.

Cutting a straight line by hand

Many of the invitation patterns have lines that are not possible to cut with a paper cutter. Follow these instructions to make straight cuts using a metal ruler and an X-Acto knife.

1. Clearly mark where the cut will begin and end. Line up a metal ruler with the line you want to cut.

2. Line up the X-Acto knife with the ruler, and cut.

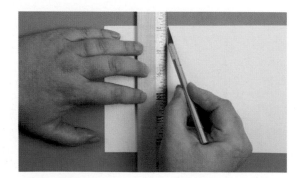

Making a crisp fold

It may seem like a small detail, but the way you fold the paper could make a big difference in the overall presentation of your invitation. Follow these instructions to make your folds look as professional as possible.

1. Line up a ruler on the desired fold. Score the desired fold with an awl.

2. Line up the edges and match the corners accurately. Smooth with a bone folder.

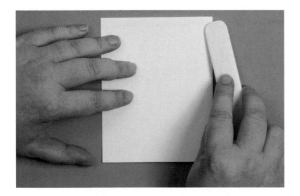

Tip

A monogram sticker placed under the vellum makes a great focal point for your invitation.

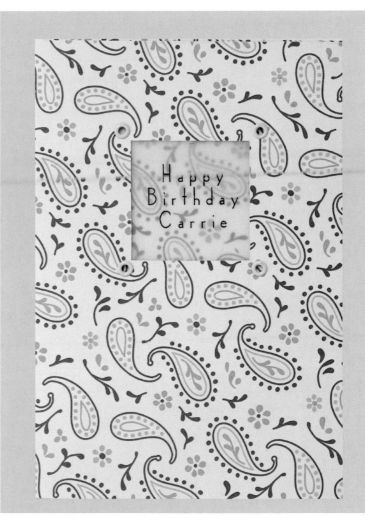

This simple trifold Invitation has so many possibilities!

More Creative folds

MR. AND MRS. STEVEN ANDERSON
ARE PLEASED TO ANNOUNCE THE MARRIAGE
OF THEIR DAUGHTER,

Christina Joyce

AND

James Daniel Smith

SON OF MR. AND MRS. GREGORY SMITH

AND REQUEST THE PLEASURE OF YOUR COMPANY
AT A RECEPTION IN THEIR HONOR

ON TUESDAY, THE TENTH OF MAY
TWO THOUSAND AND FOUR
FROM 7:00-9:30

AT THE HOME OF
BRYCE AND LINDSAY SMITH
1116 RYAN WAY ~ CLAYTON CALIFORNIA

A simple wedding invitation becomes elegant once it is placed inside this patterned vellum slide. See the pattern on the pullout.

☀ İDEA

Print your invitation with colorful inks.

Similar to a matchbook, this invitation is closed by tucking the top under a sewn-down flap. See the pattern on the pullout.

Sarah is
Over The Hill

You are invited to her
Birthday Celebration

When
October 15th
7:00-10:00

Where
Jackman's House
1557 Lyon Avenue

RSVP
Heidi
560-5849

This pattern creates a great invitation that can be sealed with a sticker and dropped in the mail without an envelope! See the pattern on the pullout .

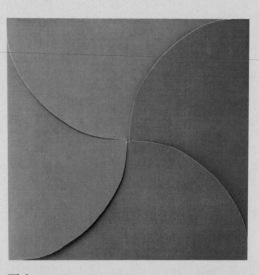

Happy Birthday
RILEY

Come Celebrate with us!

WHEN
Friday, September 24th
7:00 PM

WHERE
Our House
1437 Charleston Lane

Wrap Closures

A wrap closure is a great way to seal an invitation with a creative fold. *Turn to page 56 for directions to make your own button wrap closure.*

Making a photo easel

It is simply a trifold invitation like Happy Birthday Carrie (page 13), but one more fold turns it into an easel! Experiment with the technique on scratch paper so you can see exactly how it will fold, as well as where to put the photo and any embellishments.

1. Measure the photo you will use, and measure your cardstock accordingly. Cut your cardstock ⅓ longer than you want the resulting announcement.

2. Score 2 folds, so the card will fold in thirds.

3. Score the right third of the card so it will fold in half. The outside edge of this fold is the connecting flap.

4. Place the photo on the back of the middle section. Affix a strip of Glue Dots to the backside of the connecting flap. Be sure to leave the paper on the other side of the Glue Dots for mailing.

5. Send it flat, with all of the folds scored. Include instructions for your friends to peel off the Glue Dots paper and adhere the flap to the back of the announcement, creating an easel.

Give your guests something that will last long after the party is over: a photo mounted to its own easel.

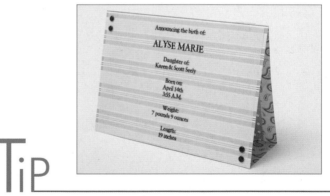

Tip

The product Glue Dots are perfect for easel announcements. They are little dabs of glue between two nonstick layers of paper. This allows you to peel off the paper to expose one side of the adhesive for you to stick on the connecting flap, while keeping the other side of the adhesive covered until the recipients are ready to construct the easel.

Announcing
the recent birth of

Jacob Brent Giles

November 6th, 2003
8 Pounds 11 ounces
21 inches

son of
Greg & Melissa Giles

Use a picture of the guest of honor or
another simple embellishment in the
window of this neat announcement.

Invitations with Creative Shapes

Each one of these invitations can be easily reproduced. Simply follow the instructions and use the patterns on the pullout. When using a pattern, remember to cut on solid lines and score on dotted lines. Here are a few tips to make your invitations with creative shapes look their best.

You can do so much with this basic purse pattern. Try adding a monogram sticker, a ribbon handle, or lace around the edges.

This is perfect for a baby shower.

come meet
HARRISON
son of Carrie & Jerom

WHEN
September 12th
at 2:30

WHERE
John & Julie's House
1438 Star Avenue

RSVP
Vicki Collette
684-5959

it's a BOY

TIPS

- When cutting a curved line, always keep the scissor tips pointed away from your body. Also, turn the paper, not the scissors, as you cut.

- To avoid tearing the paper, cut into tight angles.

- Trace a pattern onto the back of the paper with a pencil that can be easily erased.

These patterns are great to use for any school-related event.

Pencil us in...

Pine Hollow Elementary School Open House is coming soon!

Mark your calendars for:

⟡ **Wednesday, September 25th** ⟡

7:00- 9:00 P.M.

Come meet your child's teacher and learn what educational adventures await them in the upcoming school year.

come...

To a
Retirement
Open House
for:

Mrs. Irma Luebbe

When:
Friday, April 20th
at 6:00-9:00

Where:
The school library

light refreshments
will be served

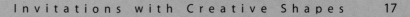

This gift pattern could be used for a variety of different parties, including a birthday or a Christmas party.

To Oscar's Birthday Party

WHEN
Saturday, June 7th
2:00- 5:00

WHERE
Our House
1285 Loma Linda St.

RSVP
Marlene
674-6567

YOU ARE INVITED

YOU ARE INVITED

You will have to plan a tea party just so you can create these fun invitations!

You are invited to a tea party in celebration of
Mag's 6th birthday

When:
Saturday, July 26th
1:00-2:00

Where:
Our Backyard Cafe
465 Garden Lane

Slide the ladybug's wings up to reveal the birthday party invitation.

START YOUR ENGINES...
IT'S GONNA BE A WILD RIDE!

YOU ARE INVITED TO
GARRETT'S BIRTHDAY PARTY

WHEN
SATURDAY, MARCH 15TH
AT 1:00

WHERE
OUR HOUSE
148 MAPLE WAY

SEE YOU THERE!

What little boy wouldn't love to get a truck invitation? Use your creativity to enhance and personalize this basic pattern. See the pattern on the pullout.

IDEA

Make your pattern by simply printing out a letter or number in a large font size.

Make your invitations in the shape of a number or letter significant to the guest of honor, such as his or her age or initial.

YOU ARE INVITED TO
A BIRTHDAY PARTY FOR
LILLIAN

WHEN
JULY 15TH
AT 6:00

BRING
A TOWEL &
SWIMSUIT

RSVP
LATRICE
485-9656

WHERE
OUR HOUSE
12 PARK AVE.

IT'S A
PARTY

COME TO A BIRTHDAY PARTY FOR SPENCER THIS SATURDAY AT 1:00 AT OUR HOUSE (1345 SUNRISE AVENUS) BRING YOUR SWIMSUIT & TOWEL!

IT'S A
PARTY

This daisy would work great for a summer birthday party. Turn to page 34 for directions on making the 3-D center.

IDEA

If you don't have computer software that allows you to position text easily, you can handwrite your invitation text or use rubber alphabet stamps on the Daisy and "5" invitations.

Embellishing
Your Invitations

Embellish with Ribbon

Y ou can add style to your invitation by using ribbon. Ribbon is available in a variety of widths, textures, colors, and patterns. Experiment with different styles to find the ribbon that best complements the colors and style of your invitation. In addition to ribbon, there are many other possibilities you can include in your invitation, such as rickrack, fabric strips, lace, fibers, twill tape, or hemp. Once you have found the perfect ribbon, use one of the following ideas to incorporate it into your invitation.

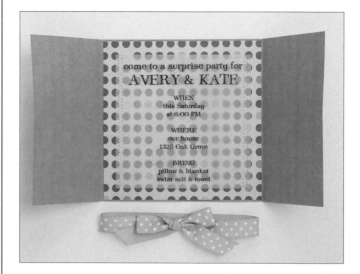

A bow wrapped around an invitation is a great way to keep it closed.

Tying a bow that lays straight

1. Make a loop in both ribbon ends.

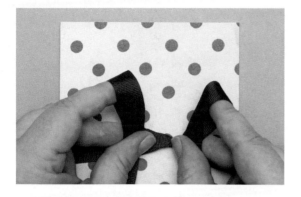

2. Tie the 2 loops together in a knot and pull tight.

Tying a secure square knot

1. Tie a knot with the right string on top.

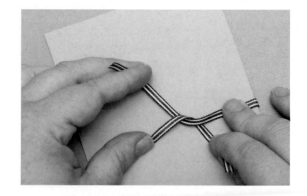

2. Tie a knot with the left string on top.

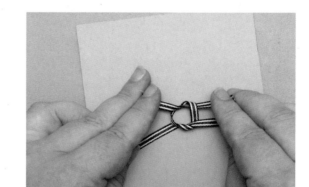

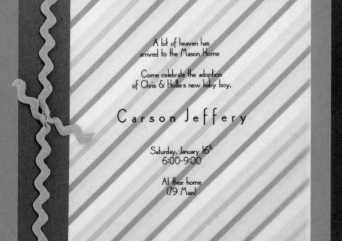

A length of rickrack tied in a simple square knot adds so much.

Connect your invitation layers with a few short ribbon ties.

Threading ribbon through a small opening

1. Use needle-nose tweezers to thread ribbon through the front of the invitation.

2. Grab the ribbon from the back of the invitation and pull through.

TiP

Do not trim the ribbon ends until your knot is secure. This will make your knot or bow much easier to tie.

IDEA

To avoid making your invitation too busy, use a multicolored ribbon with simple paper, or vice versa.

SYDNEY
is turning ten...celebrate with us

party

WHEN
Saturday, July 3rd 5:00

WHERE
1290 Rounhill Place

RSVP
634-2029

There are many creative ways to attach ribbon to your invitation, including staples!

Combine multiple ribbons to achieve a sophisticated look.

Baby DYLAN is on his way!
Come celebrate with Hillary & Ben

Saturday, November 15th
11:00-1:00

At Danielle Engstrom's House
1284 Pine Avenue

A light luncheon will be served

Regrets Only
576-9393

We welcome with love

Bryce Edward

March 25th, 2005

8 pounds 2 ounces

Sandy & Ed Wilson

A ribbon is a great embellishment for a tag invitation.

come
CHRISTMAS CAROLING
with us

WHEN
This Friday, December 22nd
at 7:00

WHERE
meet at the Rasmussens
hot cocoa at the Andersens
afterwards

BRING
3 dozen cookies to share

A fabric strip can be used like ribbon.

IDEAs

- Paint clear nail polish on the ends of your fabric strip or ribbon to prevent fraying.

- Combine ribbons with a variety of textures, colors, widths, and patterns. If they all echo colors from your invitation, they will come together.

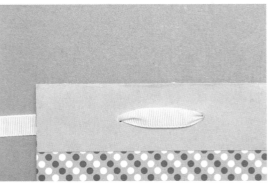

You are invited to a
Bridal Shower for:

Autumn Olsen

When:
Saturday, April 15th
2:00–4:00

Where:
Davis Residence
1439 Shadow Lane

RSVP:
Teresa Davis
295-4596

Secure your invitation with this simple threading technique.

Threading ribbon in this style

1. Thread both ends of the ribbon through the front of the invitation.

2. Thread the ribbon ends up from the back in opposite holes.

Threading ribbon in this style

1. Fold the ribbon in half.

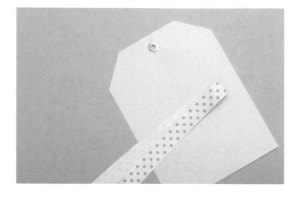

2. Thread about 2″ of the ribbon loop through the front of the eyelet.

3. Thread the 2 cut ends of the ribbon through the ribbon loop.

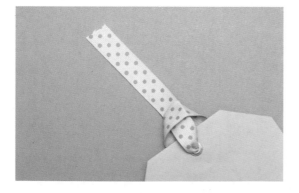

4. Pull tight.

Thread a tag or other embellishment through your ribbon before tying it off.

Embellish with Eyelets and Brads

Eyelets and brads are both functional and decorative. They are an effective way to keep layers of paper in place and can be a great embellishment for your invitations. Because they are available in a range of colors, shapes, and sizes, you are sure to find something perfect for your invitation. Look to the following examples for inspiration for fresh ways to incorporate them into your invitations.

Eyelets with printed letters can be used to spell out a word on your invitation.

Using an eyelet setter

1. Punch a hole at the marked location.

2. Put an eyelet into the hole.

3. Turn the invitation and eyelet over and hammer the eyelet with an eyelet setter until the eyelet prongs are folded over.

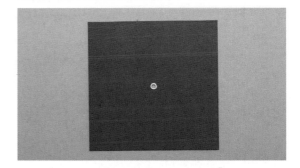

4. The eyelet should attach smoothly to your invitation.

Tip

When figuring out how to center eyelets, first find the center of your invitation. Then measure equal distances on either side of the center eyelet to determine where to attach the other eyelets.

Attaching a brad

1. Locate and mark where you want to attach the brad.

2. Poke a hole with an awl.

3. Slide the brad into the hole.

4. Bend the brad prongs open on the backside of the paper.

TiP

To easily find the center of an invitation, cut a strip of paper the same width as the invitation. Fold this strip in half and you'll find the center.

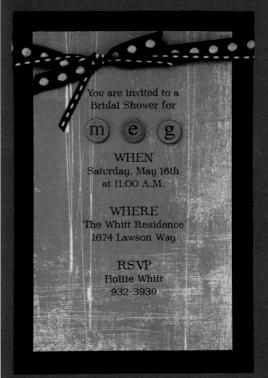

You are invited to a
Bridal Shower for

m **e** **g**

WHEN
Saturday, May 16th
at 11:00 A.M.

WHERE
The Whitt Residence
1674 Lawson Way

RSVP
Hollie Whitt
932-3939

Eyelets don't have to be used only at the top of an invitation. Try securing decorative eyelets in the center of your invitation.

You are invited to a
BABY SHOWER
for Shannon Powell
& baby Conner

WHEN
Saturday, February 4th
at 11:30 A.M.

WHERE
Courtney Powell's Home
1230 Discovery Way

RSVP
Natalie Seely
345-5454

Three decorative brads attached off-center add an interesting touch to this invitation.

You are invited to:

**Zachary's
Birthday Party!**

When:
Saturday, November 3rd
11:00-2:00

Where:
At His House
1986 Hidden Lane

RSVP:
672-7688

Paper strips and eyelets keep this vellum secure, while also serving as creative embellishments.

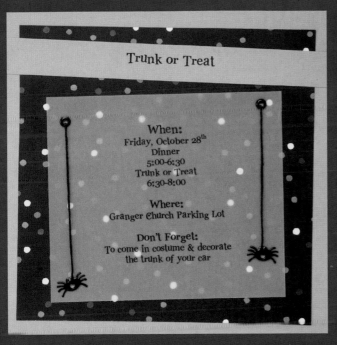

Trunk or Treat

When:
Friday, October 28th
Dinner
5:00-6:30
Trunk or Treat
6:30-8:00

Where:
Granger Church Parking Lot

Don't Forget:
To come in costume & decorate
the trunk of your car

Decorative spider eyelets were used as a great embellishment for this invitation.

Come to a
birthday party for

A l i c e

WHEN
Saturday, April 15th
7:00-12:00

WHERE
Our House
1368 Main St

sweet
sixteen

HAPPY BIRTHDAY
JAYDEN

Come celebrate with us!

WHEN
Saturday, March 13th
at 1:00 P.M.

WHERE
James Park Pool
1430 Lemon Avenue

BRING
swimsuit & towel

SEE YOU THEN!

A row of snaps holds the embellishment on this invitation in place.

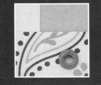

Four eyelets were used on this invitation as a simple way to hold the pocket in place.

Come to a
birthday party for

sweet
sixteen

✿ IDEA

With so many different eyelets available, you should be able to find shaped eyelets perfect for your invitation.

 Eyelets are available in many decorative shapes, themes, and sizes. Look for an eyelet that is perfect for your invitation theme. Also, use sandpaper to give your paper a weathered, rugged look.

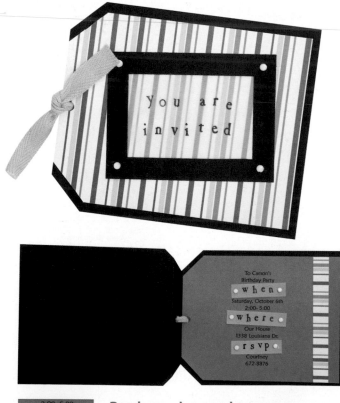

 Brads can be used to secure any element of your invitation, including the text.

Embellish with Sewing

Sewing is a creative way to hold your invitation together securely. Use a thread color that complements the invitation. There are many different ways you can sew your invitation: You can machine sew a single straight stitch, a double straight stitch, or even a zigzag. You could also try sewing a stitch by hand. Look through the following invitations for sewing technique ideas.

Machine sewing on paper

1. Leave a couple of inches of thread before you begin sewing.

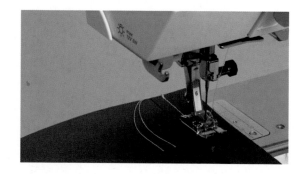

2. Backstitch at the beginning and end of your sewing.

3. Leave another couple of inches of thread at the end of your sewing.

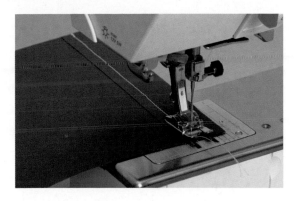

4. Glue the extra thread on both sides of the stitching to the back of the invitation. This will prevent the stitches from unraveling.

5. Hide the back of the stitches. (Refer to the instructions on page 30.)

Hand sewing a straight stitch on paper

1. Draw a light pencil line where you want to stitch.

2. Measure and mark every ¼". Poke holes in these marks with an awl.

3. Tie the thread off with a knot.

4. Sew up and down alternately through every hole.

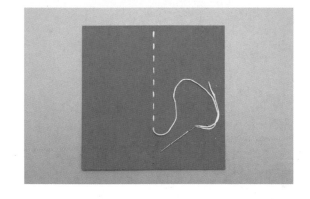

5. When the stitching is complete, secure with a square knot.

6. Hide the back of the stitches and thread ends. (Refer to the instructions on page 30.)

Hiding the back of your stitches

1. Cut your invitation twice as long as you want it to end up.

2. When you have completed your sewing, score and fold over the extra length.

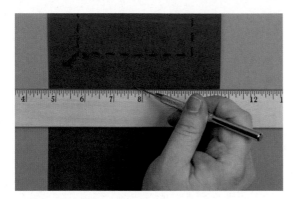

3. Secure in place with glue.

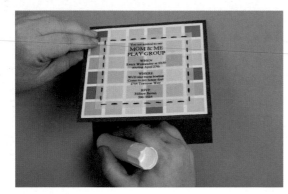

IDEA

Using a zigzag stitch on an invitation is fun!

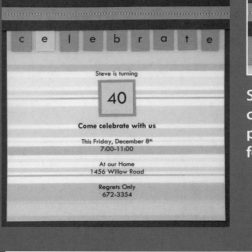

Sew on a contrasting paper strip for interest.

Hand sew a straight stitch to attach and embellish. To achieve this look, begin stitching on both sides. Where the two ends meet, secure with a bow.

YOU ARE INVITED TO A
SURPRISE BIRTHDAY PARTY FOR

MADISON

WHEN
SATURDAY, MARCH 10TH
AT 1:00

WHERE
THE WERTZ' HOME
1226 PETERSON WAY

RSVP
JESSICA
674-5352

13

Sew around the entire invitation both to hold it in place and as an embellishment.

Announcing
the arrival of

Brianna Rose

Daughter of
Sylvia & Michael Clark

Born
December 30ᵗʰ
12:57 PM

Weighing
6 pounds 4 ounces

Measuring
19 inches

BABY FACE

Two rows of stitching create a fun accent.

celebrate

with Tyler on his
BIRTHDAY!

WHEN
June 20th
2:00

WHERE
Bradley Park

RSVP
672-4949

SEE YOU THEN!

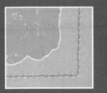

Sew vellum onto the top of the invitation. Tear out the center, and you will end up with a unique border.

Your family is invited to a

Farewell
Open House

for the Taylor Family

When
Sunday, May 21ˢᵗ
5:00-8:00

Where
White Residence
1234 Willow Lane

Bring
A family picture to
put into a scrapbook for them

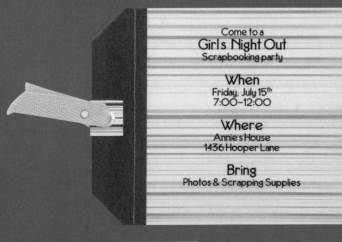

Come to a
Girls Night Out
Scrapbooking party

When
Friday, July 15ᵗʰ
7:00–12:00

Where
Annie's House
1436 Hooper Lane

Bring
Photos & Scrapping Supplies

A simple straight stitch can be a great embellishment.

Your family is invited to a

Farewell
Open House

for the Taylor Family

Sewing is a fun and secure way to keep a pocket in place.

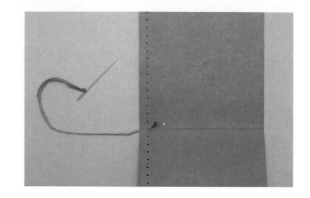

Attach a pocket with a hand-sewn whipstitch.

2. With a pocket invitation, start your first stitch on the inside of the pocket to conceal the knot.

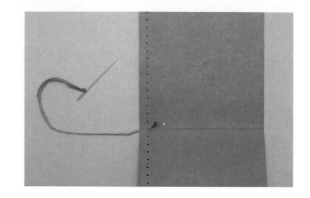

3. Stitch around the edge of the invitation and up through the next hole.

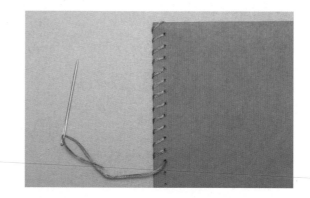

4. Finish the sewing and tie a knot on the inside of the pocket to hide it. Trim the thread close to the knot.

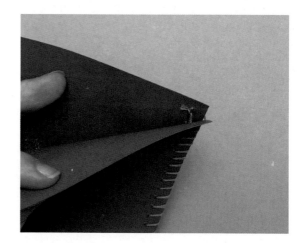

Sewing a whipstitch

1. Draw a light pencil line where you want to stitch (1/4″ from the edge of the invitation). Measure and mark every 1/4″. Poke holes in these marks with an awl.

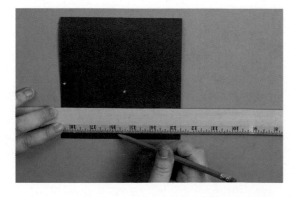

Embellish with Patterned Paper

I am amazed at how many different patterned paper designs are available! You can find patterned paper in virtually every color and style imaginable. Be inspired by these techniques, and incorporate patterned paper into your invitations in a creative way.

Stella is turning 4!
come celebrate with us

WHEN,
Saturday, May 3rd at 11:00

WHERE
1620 Raspberry Circle

RSVP
576-8787

Cut a design from patterned paper. Frame it on a tag for a great coordinating embellishment.

Centering your design in a tag

1. Cut a circle out of vellum the same size as the inside of the tag.

2. Place that vellum circle on your patterned paper.

3. When you have the design aligned the way you want it, trace the circle and cut it out.

You are invited
to the annual neighborhood

EASTER
EGG HUNT

WHEN
Saturday, March 26th
1:00 P.M.

WHERE
Hindley Park
1750 Tulip Place

BRING
Picnic Lunch for your family
15 filled plastic eggs per child

Frame a design cut from patterned paper, turning the paper into an embellishment. I used a concho here.

Making a dimensional embellishment

1. Cut out the design.

2. Glue the design onto heavy board. (The board found on the back of a paper tablet works great.)

3. When the glue is dry, cut around the design with an X-Acto knife.

4. Sand the edges to make your embellishment smooth.

5. Apply a matching color of fluid chalk ink to the edges of the embellishment. The ink will add a weathered look to your embellishment. It will also hide the edges of the heavy board.

 You can make almost any basic shape with patterned paper that matches your invitation. To make the shape dimensional, follow the instructions at left.

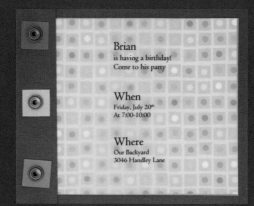

 Repeat shapes and colors from your patterned paper to create a great embellishment.

BRYNNE
IS TURNING 5

come to her party

WHEN
March 27th at 1:00

WHERE
1536 Park Avenue

RSVP
384-5954

Hailey is turning five!

Come have a "berry" good time with us...

Saturday, September 27th
At 1:00 p.m.

Meet at our house
(1338 Country Lane)

Bring your swim suit!

Add dimension to your embellishment by mounting it on solid cardboard.

Tear patterned paper into basic shapes to make an embellishment for your invitation.

HAPPY BIRTHDAY
JESSICA!

come celebrate with us

WHEN
Saturday, April 6th
at 1:00

WHERE
Mary Hardy's House
1823 Rosedall Place

RSVP
Jeri Harvard
496-4545

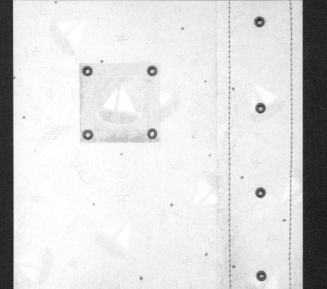

Using the technique described on page 34, create a gift embellishment with patterned paper. The ribbon on the gift is also used to seal the invitation.

The boat was cut from patterned paper and mounted on solid cardstock to make a great embellishment for this invitation.

A premade scrapbook frame works great as a frame around an invitation.

Embellish with Premade Artwork

There are many great scrapbooking and craft products available. If you are short on time or creativity, use a premade embellishment to add a lot of style and emphasize the theme of your invitation.

Make your own personalized patterned paper using your computer or rubber stamps.

Photo by Hillary Bevan

Several coordinating die cuts are used together to create a unique embellishment.

BUZZ
on over for an afternoon of

S U M M E R   F U N !

At
Mrs. Thompson's
1435 Lilac Way

On
June 21ˢᵗ
At 11:00

Bring
Your swim gear
& an appetite!

Three of the same illustration are used together to create a great embellishment for this invitation.

A premade 3-D embellishment can add a lot to an invitation. The duckling's velvety texture is echoed by a ribbon with a similar texture.

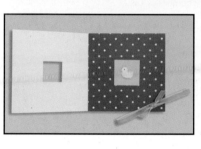

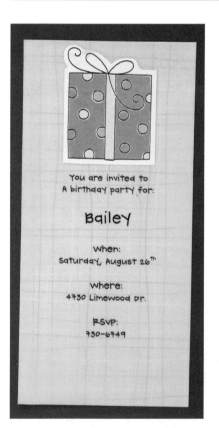

You are invited to
A birthday party for:

Bailey

when:
Saturday, August 26ᵗʰ

where:
4730 Limewood Dr.

RSVP:
730-6749

Foam squares are used to attach this die cut. The squares hold very securely and also add some dimension to the die cut.

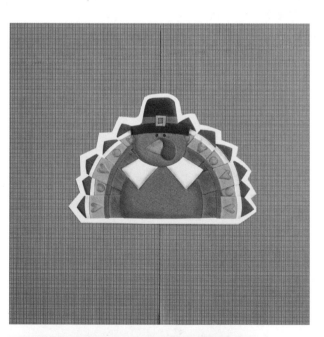

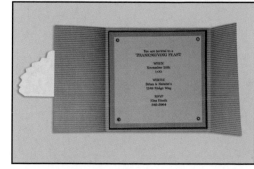

The left side of the turkey was glued to only the left flap of the invitation.

Happy Mother's Day!

You are invited to a luncheon
prepared by your son or daughter

When
Friday, May 7th
1:00-2:30

Where
Clyde Memorial Elementary
Mrs. Jacksons classroom (B-5)

RSVP
Before May 5th
486-4945

TEAM PARTY!

WHEN: THIS SATURDAY, DECEMBER 8TH
          6:00- 8:00

WHERE: PATTI'S PIZZA SHACK
          1134 MORTENSEN BLVD.

RSVP: CRAIG COLLETTE
          495-6656

BRING: MONEY FOR THE COACH NED'S GIFT

This daisy die cut is perfect for a Mother's Day invitation. With so many die cuts available, you shouldn't have a problem finding one perfect for your invitation.

The colors and textures from the baseball embellishments are echoed in the paper used for this invitation.

BIRTHDAY GIRL

A die cut meant for a scrapbook page title can be a neat embellishment.

You are invited to a
PARTY for KAYLA

WHEN
February 12th
11:30

WHERE
Kid Center
1183 Highland St.

RSVP
Olivia
472-5345

Your family
is invited to our annual

4th of July
Pancake Breakfast

When:
July 4th
9:00-11:00 A.M

Where:
Carrington
Meeting House

A die cut can be a fun background on an invitation printed on vellum.

HAPPY BIRTHDAY BROOKLYN

Attach a premade embellishment to your invitation in a creative way.

Embellish with Photos

A great way to personalize an invitation or announcement is to include a photograph of the guest of honor. The photograph will be a gift to your guest that will last long after the party is over. Look through the following examples for ideas on how to include a photograph with your invitation.

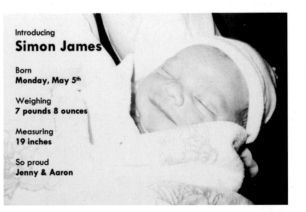

Print your invitation directly onto a photograph.

IDEA

This is simply done by running a photo through your computer printer, following the manufacturer's instructions. A picture with a large white area works best for readability.

Centering a photo within a tag

1. Cut a vellum square the size of the inside of the tag.

2. Center the vellum square over the picture, moving it around until it is positioned over the exact part of the photograph you want to feature.

3. Once you have decided where you want to cut the picture, trace around the vellum square.

4. Cut out the picture.

A photograph placed under a vellum announcement makes a great background.

A large tag was used to frame this picture.

This invitation style makes a great frame for a photograph.

A window cut out of vellum will make the guest of honor the focal point of the announcement.

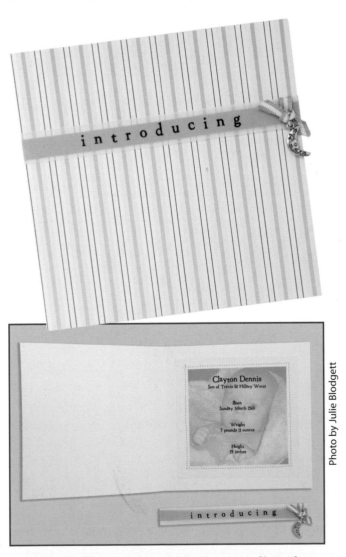

A vellum announcement was sewn directly over a great picture of the guest of honor.

A vellum wraparound was used to keep the picture and invitation together.

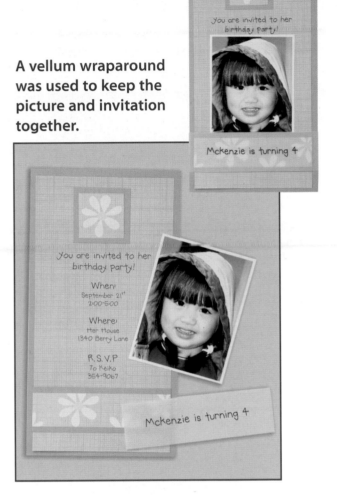

A mini scrapbook page with the party information instead of journaling can be a fun invitation.

The vellum-printed invitation allows a view of the cute picture inside.

Embellish with Other Finds

Browse your local craft, hardware, or dollar store for small embellishments that could be incorporated into your invitations. Don't be afraid to experiment with unexpected materials. Have certain colors and a theme in mind, to keep from feeling overwhelmed. When mailing your invitations, remember that embellishments can add bulk and may require additional postage.

A fun frame was made for this picture by tearing the edges of paper layers and sewing them together.

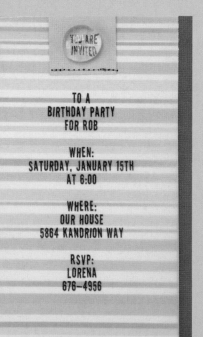

A clear pebble placed on the invitation magnifies the headline and makes it stand out.

You are invited to a
Birthday Party for:

Avery

When:
Saturday
December 8th

At:
Our House
1530 Aspen Way

RSVP:
Jill Collette
809-7050

A single jewel is a great embellishment for an invitation.

IDEA

Connect the vellum to the other paper layers with a Glue Dot cleverly positioned directly under the jewel.

A mini pacifier is tied onto a wraparound for this baby announcement.

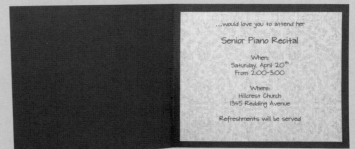

Boy oh boy!

Ethan Davis

Came into the world
on March 3rd, 2002

weighing:
8 pounds 9 ounces

measuring:
20 inches

parents:
Ned & Jean Lee

...would love you to attend her

Senior Piano Recital

When:
Saturday, April 20th
From 2:00-3:00

Where:
Hillcrest Church
1345 Redding Avenue

Refreshments will be served

Charms can add variety and style to your invitation.

IDEA

A line printed around the invitation can be a great border.

JOSHUA & JOEY

ARRIVED
August 16th
10:15 A.M.

WEIGHING
5 pounds 6 ounces
5 pounds 4 ounces

MEASURING
17 inches
16 1/2 inches

PROUD PARENTS
Jeni & Jake Harward

A diaper pin embellished with colorful beads is used to creatively attach the layers.

50 Brandon Jones is having a birthday

When: Friday, June 2nd
7:00pm

Where: Our Home
7345 Juniper Drive

RSVP: Lauren Johnson
392-9785

come celebrate with us

A decorative paper clip is a quick, casual, and sometimes masculine solution to hold an invitation together.

Tip

Uncoil the diaper pin slightly to put beads on it.

IDEA

A simple "X" stitch can be used to hold your invitation together.

A tag is a very "in" thing to include.

IDEA

When stamping a word in a certain amount of space, such as on a tag, stamp the middle letter of the word first, then stamp the other letters of the word on either side. This will help you space the letters evenly.

A silk flower can be a fun, inexpensive embellishment.

You are invited to a birthday party for

SADIE

WHEN
Saturday, March 10th
2:00

WHERE
Cano Park
1854 Clayton Road

RSVP
Dora
865-3434

Embellish with an Enhanced Word

There are many innovative scrapbooking and craft products available with letters printed on them, including beads, eyelets, charms, stickers, metal charms, and so on. Use these products to spell out and highlight a word on your invitation. This is a great way to personalize your invitation and make it unique. You can also play with different fonts and font effects on your computer to highlight a single word on your invitation. There are endless possibilities of words you can enhance on your invitations.

Here are a few headline suggestions:

- The name or initials of the guest of honor
- The age of the guest of honor (for a birthday)
- Celebrate
- (It's a) Party
- You Are (Cordially) Invited
- (Please) Come
- It's a Surprise!
- Birthday (Party)
- Here Comes the Bride (bridal shower)
- It's a Boy/Girl!
- Love (wedding shower)
- Merry (Christmas party)
- Boo! (Halloween party)
- Hot (summer bash)
- Mark Your Calendar

Make your invitation more meaningful with a quote.

LGC invitation
Craig & Penny Collette
are pleased to announce the
birth of their daughter.

Lauren Grace

November 3rd, 2005
2:06 A.M.

6 pounds 13 ounces
20 inches

LUCY invitation
IS TURNING 9!
Come celebrate with us

WHEN:
Saturday, June 15th

WHERE:
Our Backyard
1453 Limewood Lane

RSVP:
456-9030

Jack invitation
is turning

10

Come to his

**Surprise
Birthday Party**

When:
Friday, January 26th
6:00-11:00

Where:
At our home
7860 Wyatt Lane

The emphasized initials of the guest of honor make a distinctive embellishment.

Use a creative format to spell a word you want to stand out.

Attach letters to the invitation before securing the fold-over.

Individual letters can be hung from eyelets to spell out a word.

To a baby shower for:

Claire Mason

when:
Saturday, January 20th
10:30-12:30

where:
6723 Meadow view circle

A light brunch will be served

R.S.V.P:
Kelly McKissik
687-9090

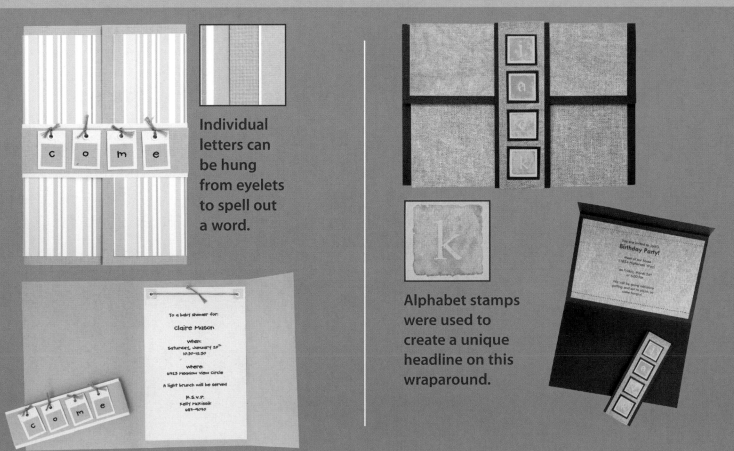

Alphabet stamps were used to create a unique headline on this wraparound.

You are invited to Jack's
Birthday Party!

Meet at our house
11854 Highcrest Way

on Friday, March 26th
at 5:00 P.m.

We will be going miniature
golfing and out to pizza, so
come hungry!

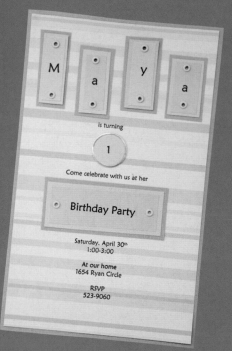

is turning

1

Come celebrate with us at her

Birthday Party

Saturday, April 30th
1:00-3:00

At our home
1654 Ryan Circle

RSVP
523-9060

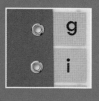

Individual letters or words can be secured with eyelets.

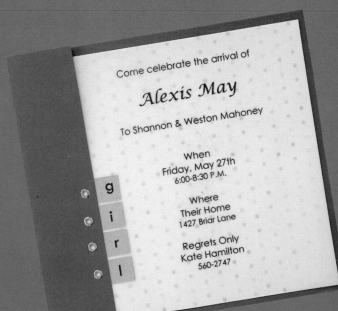

Come celebrate the arrival of

Alexis May

To Shannon & Weston Mahoney

When
Friday, May 27th
6:00-8:30 P.M.

Where
Their Home
1427 Briar Lane

Regrets Only
Kate Hamilton
560-2747

Paper strips with printed letters were glued in place before the folded-over edge was glued down. Eyelets were used both as an embellishment and to keep the paper strips from shifting.

Embellish with Buttons

Visit the notions aisle in your local craft or sewing supply store and you will be amazed at how many different buttons exist. Surely you should be able to find the perfect button in the perfect color and shape to embellish your invitation. Sometimes a single button is best, but experiment with multiple buttons and the patterns you can create with a variety of different colored and shaped buttons. You can adhere a button with strong glue (such as mono-adhesive or hot glue) or sew it onto the invitation with thread, hemp, or string.

Sewing a button onto paper

1. Decide where you want to attach the button to your invitation.

2. Place the button on your invitation and use a pencil to mark the buttonholes.

3. Remove the button and poke holes on the marks with an awl.

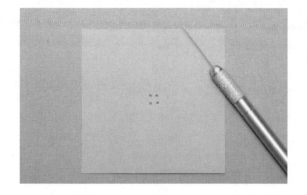

4. Replace the button. Attach it by sewing down through the top of one hole on the button and up through the other hole.

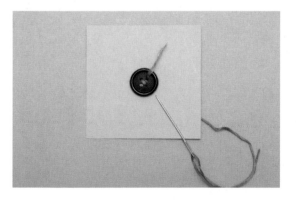

5. Tie the string ends off with a square knot or bow.

Tip

A button that has a shank rather than holes can fit into a slit made with an X-Acto knife and can be secured in place with hot glue.

A leather button is a classy embellishment.

Come to our
BOOK CLUB

WHEN
January 16th
at 7:00 PM

WHERE
Shelly Crams House
1546 Dyson Way

BRING
A favorite
book suggestion

RSVP
Julie Lake
793-0567

A "button wrap" makes a great seal.

Tip

To make this style invitation, first sew the button onto the invitation, leaving a long piece of string. Then attach that piece of string to the invitation sleeve through an eyelet. Finally, cut out a space in the sleeve for the button to fit into. See the sleeve pattern on the pullout. You can modify this to fit any size invitation.

A button is used to attach the layers and also to attach the invitation to a pocket.

Tip

You can find instructions to make a button wrap on page 56.

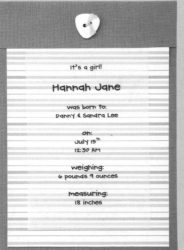

It's a girl!

Hannah Jane

was born to:
Danny & Sandra Lee

on:
July 15th
12:30 AM

weighing:
6 pounds 9 ounces

measuring:
18 inches

A button with an interesting shape adds to the fun style.

She is cute as a button!

Annalyse Hartman

Came into the world
December 30th

Weighing
5 pounds 10 ounces

Measuring
18 inches

Belonging to
James & Sylvia

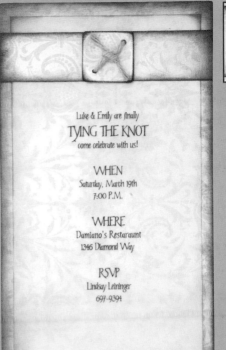

Luke & Emily are finally
TYING THE KNOT
come celebrate with us!

WHEN
Saturday, March 19th
7:00 P.M.

WHERE
Damiano's Restaraunt
1346 Diamond Way

RSVP
Lindsay Leininger
697-9394

Make your own matching "button."

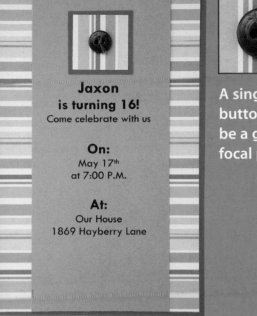

Jaxon
is turning 16!
Come celebrate with us

On:
May 17th
at 7:00 P.M.

At:
Our House
1869 Hayberry Lane

A single button can be a great focal point.

Tip

To make your own "button," follow the Dimensional Embellishment instructions on page 34. Use an awl to make the buttonholes. Secure it in place by sewing, as if it were a real button.

Celebrate the retirement of

Samantha Clark

WHEN

July 25th
7:30-10:30

WHERE

Garden Park
1548 Vine Boulevard

RSVP

Janice Nielsen
563-5869

Three buttons make a great embellishment.

HAPPY BIRTHDAY PAM!

come celebrate with us

WHEN
April 2nd
at 6:00.

WHERE
Marissa's House
1345 Olsen Way

RSVP
Marilyn
578-3934

Two buttons were used to hold this headline in place. They serve their purpose well and are also a great embellishment.

Envelopes

Envelopes

The first part of the invitation that your guest will see is the envelope. Take the time to consider what envelope will best complement the invitation. You can add a simple embellishment to make the envelope more interesting. If you prefer, you can make your own envelopes out of virtually any material using the pattern on the pullout. Be inspired by these samples and create an envelope worthy of your great handmade invitation.

Print embellished addresses directly onto the envelopes with your computer printer.

Tip

If you can't achieve the embellished address with your software, run the envelopes through your printer twice: once to print the light monogram and a second time to print the address.

Tip

There are many different shapes you could cut out of your envelope to allow the address to show through. Use a die cut or large punch, or get unique results with an X-Acto knife, scissors, or hand tearing.

A transparent envelope provides an exciting glimpse of a special event. It also provides more creative addressing possibilities.

Stamp or print words onto your envelope to give your guests a hint of the contents.

Make your own address window.

Lining your envelopes

1. Cut a piece of patterned paper ¼″ narrower than the width of your envelope and the height of the envelope from the bottom to just under the gummed strip.

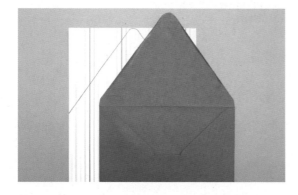

2. Slide the trimmed patterned paper into the envelope. Use a light table (or sunlight through a window!) and lightly trace a silhouette ⅛″ inside the envelope edge.

3. Remove the paper and cut along this line. Slide the patterned paper back into the envelope.

4. Fold down the envelope flap.

5. Slide a piece of scratch paper under the lining and run a glue stick over the back of the lining.

6. Press the glued lining back onto the envelope flap to attach.

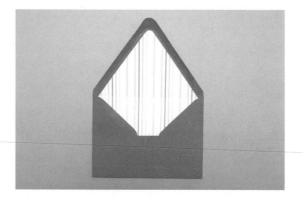

Line your envelopes with a coordinating patterned paper.

A vellum envelope can show off a fun photograph, even before your guest opens the envelope. See the pattern on the pullout.

mildred & daryl peterson · 485 state street · atlanta, georgia · 73535

Seal the envelope or a creatively folded invitation with a classy return address label.

Emily Leininger
123 Main Street
Oakland, California
98005

Make your own creative envelope seals. Echo the colors, fonts, and style of your invitation.

Enhance your envelope with a button wrap

1. Cut or punch two ¾″ circles out of contrasting cardstock.

2. Glue the circles in the center of your envelope, one just above and one just below your flap.

3. Secure in place with eyelets in the center of each circle.

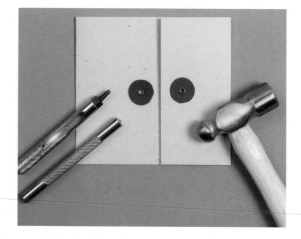

4. Tie a slipknot into the string to be used for the wrapping.

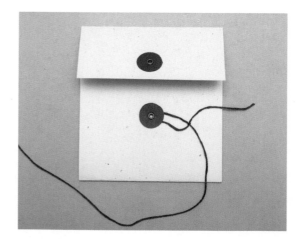

5. Slip the loose knot around one of the buttons.

6. Once the string is in place, tighten the slipknot and tie a second knot to secure the string.

7. Trim the string and wrap it around the eyelets.

I hope that these pages spark your creativity and inspire you to make announcements for any upcoming event. Now you are ready to make invitations that you should be excited and proud to send to your guests!

Supply Sources

Introduction

KARLEE
Brown paper: Provo Craft
Pink paper: Making Memories
Patterned paper: Making
 Memories
Vellum: Provo Craft
Font: 2Peas Tubby
Charm: Marian & Me
Ribbon: May Arts

GREGORY
Solid paper: Provo Craft
Patterned paper: S.E.I.
Vellum: Provo Craft
Font: 2Peas Tasklist
Hemp: May Arts
Tag: Making Memories
Monogram charm: Unknown

PORTER DANIEL
Solid paper: Provo Craft
Patterned paper: Basic Grey
Vellum: Provo Craft
Font: 2Peas Renaissance
Ribbon: All My Memories
Frame: Making Memories

Invitations with a Fold-Over

JAYDEN
Solid paper: Provo Craft
Patterned paper: S.E.I.
Vellum: Provo Craft
Fonts: Tw Cen MT, 2Peas Duck
 Duck Goose
Tacks: Chatterbox

Invitations with a Pocket

ALEXANDRA'S SLUMBER PARTY
Solid paper: Provo Craft
Patterned paper: KI Memories
Font: 2Peas Renaissance

Invitations with a Wraparound

APRIL OLIVER
Solid paper: Bazzill Basics
Patterned paper: S.E.I.
Vellum: Provo Craft
Font: 2Peas Sailboat
Brad: Provo Craft

COMPANY CHRISTMAS PARTY
Solid paper: Bazzill Basics
Patterned paper: Unknown
Vellum: Provo Craft
Font: AL Handcrafted
Silver eyelets: Making Memories
"Merry Christmas" eyelet:
 Making Memories

HAPPY BIRTHDAY SOPHIA
Solid paper: Provo Craft
Patterned paper: Scrapworks
Vellum: Provo Craft
Font: 2Peas Renaissance
"Happy Birthday" brad: Marian
 & Me
Photo anchors: Making Memories
Snaps: Making Memories

Invitations with Creative Folds

HAPPY BIRTHDAY CARRIE
Patterned paper: Making
 Memories
Vellum: Provo Craft
Font: 2Peas Sailboat
Eyelets: Doodlebug

FORMAL WEDDING
Solid paper: Provo Craft
Floral vellum: Unknown
Fonts: Centaur, AL Constitution

OVER THE HILL
Solid paper: Bazzill Basics
Patterned paper: S.E.I.
Vellum: Provo Craft
Font: 2Peas Tubby
Eyelets: Doodlebug
Ribbon: May Arts

RILEY
Solid paper: Chatterbox
Patterned paper: S.E.I.
Vellum: Provo Craft
Font: Centaur
Tacks: Chatterbox

GLORIA
Patterned paper: American Crafts
Vellum: Provo Craft
Font: Maiandra GD
Eyelets: Making Memories
Brads: Provo Craft
Monogram sticker: American Crafts
Hemp: May Arts

ALYSE MARIE
Photograph: Hillary Bevan
Patterned paper: My Mind's Eye
Vellum: Provo Craft
Font: 2Peas Renaissance
Dotlets: Doodlebug
Ribbon: Unknown
Heart ribbon slide: All My
 Memories

JACOB BRENT
Patterned paper: Making
 Memories
Vellum: Provo Craft
White mini brads: Provo Craft
Font: 2Peas Sailboat
Ribbon: Jolee's Boutique

Invitations with Creative Shapes

PURSE
Solid paper: Provo Craft
Patterned paper: Making
 Memories
Vellum: Provo Craft
Font: CK Plain Jane
Eyelets: Making Memories
Button: Unknown
Velcro Sticky Back coins: Velcro

BABY BOTTLE
Solid paper: Provo Craft
Patterned paper: Making
 Memories
Font: 2Peas Sailboat
Ribbon: Offray
Tag: Making Memories

PENCIL US IN
Solid brown paper: Provo Craft
Patterned pink, gray, brown,
 yellow paper: Chatterbox
Font: Tw Cen MT
Eyelets: Making Memories

APPLE
Red patterned paper: Lasting
 Impressions
Green textured paper: Unknown
Corrugated paper: Unknown
Red brad: Provo Craft
Stamps: Hero Arts
Font: 2Peas Renaissance

GIFT
Patterned paper: Treehouse
 Memories
Vellum: Provo Craft
Font: AL Handcrafted
Twill tape: May Arts
Tag: Making Memories

TEAPOT
Patterned paper: K&Company
Vellum: Provo Craft
Font: CK Whirl

LADYBUG
Solid paper: Provo Craft
Patterned paper: Lasting
 Impressions
Vellum: Provo Craft
Font: CK Higgins Handprint
Brad: The Happy Hammer
Wire: Making Memories

TRUCK
Solid blue paper: Provo Craft
Patterned paper: KI Memories
Black corrugated paper: Unknown
Silver paper: Unknown
Font: 2Peas Tasklist

DAISY
Patterned paper: Treehouse
 Memories
Vellum: Provo Craft
Fluid chalk ink: ColorBox
Font: 2Peas Tasklist

"5"
Patterned paper: S.E.I.
Font: AL Highlight
Rickrack: All My Memories
Tag: Making Memories

Embellish with Ribbon

AVERY & KATE
Patterned paper: Scrapworks
Vellum: Provo Craft
Font: AL Handcrafted
Ribbon: Unknown

CARSON JEFFERY
Patterned paper: Making
 Memories
Vellum: Provo Craft
Font: 2Peas Sailboat
Rickrack: All My Memories

OVER THE HILL SURPRISE
Solid paper: Provo Craft
Patterned paper: Scenic Route
 Paper Co.
Vellum: Provo Craft
Font: 2Peas Tubby
Ribbon: May Arts

HAPPY BIRTHDAY LEXI
Solid paper: Treehouse Memories
Patterned paper: Treehouse
 Memories
Vellum: Provo Craft
Font: 2Peas Sailboat
Ribbon: May Arts

SYDNEY
Patterned paper: Basic Grey
Font: AL Handcrafted
Ribbon: May Arts
Letters: Li'l Davis Designs

DYLAN
Solid brown paper: Provo Craft
Solid blue and patterned papers:
 Making Memories
Font: 2Peas Sailboat
Ribbon and twill tape: May Arts
Fibers: Pebbles Inc.
Charm: Marian & Me

BRYCE EDWARD
"Leather" paper: Paper
 Adventures
Patterned paper: S.E.I.
Vellum: Provo Craft
Font: 2Peas Sailboat
Eyelet: Making Memories
Twill tape: May Arts

CHRISTMAS CAROLING
Solid paper: Provo Craft
Patterned paper: Treehouse
   Memories
Vellum: Provo Craft
Font: AL Handcrafted
Fabric strip: Unknown

AUTUMN OLSEN
Solid paper: Bazzill Basics
Patterned paper: S.E.I.
Vellum: Provo Craft
Font: 2Peas Tubby
Ribbon: Offray

BRIDAL SHOWER
Solid paper: Provo Craft
Patterned paper: Basic Grey
Vellum: Provo Craft
Font: 2Peas Renaissance
Eyelets: Making Memories
Ribbon: May Arts
Tag: Making Memories

Embellish with Eyelets and Brads

TWO
Solid paper: Bazzill Basics
Patterned paper: Chatterbox
Vellum: Provo Craft
Font: CK Simple
Letter eyelets: Making Memories
Daisy eyelets: Doodlebug

BABY SHOWER
Solid paper: Provo Craft
Fonts: 2Peas Sailboat, 2Peas
   Tubby
Daisy brads: Unknown

MEG
Solid black paper: Provo Craft
Patterned paper: Basic Grey
Font: AL Handcrafted
Letter eyelets: Making Memories
Ribbon: May Arts

ZACHARY
Solid paper: Provo Craft
Patterned paper: KI Memories
Vellum: Provo Craft
Font: Century Gothic
Eyelets: Doodlebug

TRUNK OR TREAT
Solid paper: Bazzill Basics
Patterned paper: Doodlebug
Vellum: Provo Craft
Font: 2Peas Chestnuts
Black eyelets: Doodlebug
Spider eyelets: The Happy
   Hammer
Embroidery floss: DMC

JAYDEN II
Patterned paper: Treehouse
   Memories
Vellum: Provo Craft
Font: AL Handcrafted
Tacks: Chatterbox

SWEET SIXTEEN
Solid paper: Provo Craft
Patterned paper: Making
   Memories
Vellum: Provo Craft
Font: 2Peas Chestnuts
Eyelets: Doodlebug

TEAM PARTY
Solid paper: Treehouse Memories
Patterned paper: Treehouse
   Memories
Vellum: Provo Craft
Font: Impact
Soccer ball eyelet: Making
   Memories
Sandpaper: Unknown

YOU ARE INVITED
Solid paper: Provo Craft
Patterned paper: Treehouse
   Memories
Vellum: Provo Craft
Font: Maiandra GD
White mini brads: Bazzill Basics
Stamps: Hero Arts

Embellish with Sewing

CELEBRATE
Solid paper: Bazzill Basics
Patterned paper: S.E.I.
Vellum: Provo Craft
Font: Tw Cen MT

ANNOUNCING
Solid paper: Bazzill Basics
Patterned paper: S.E.I.
Font: CK Handprint
Eyelet: Making Memories
Embroidery floss: DMC

MADISON
Solid paper: Provo Craft
Patterned paper: Lasting
   Impressions
Font: 2Peas Tasklist
Snap and tag: Making Memories
Stamps: Hero Arts

BRIANNA ROSE
Solid paper: Bazzill Basics
Patterned paper: S.E.I.
Vellum: Provo Craft
Font: 2Peas Sailboat
Woven label: Me & My Big Ideas

CELEBRATE
Patterned paper: Basic Grey
Vellum: Provo Craft
Font: AL Handcrafted
Sticker: K&Company

GIRLS' NIGHT OUT
Patterned paper: Making
   Memories
Vellum: Provo Craft
Font: 2Peas Tubby
Silver eyelet: Making Memories
White mini brad: The Happy
   Hammer
Twill tape: May Arts

FAREWELL OPEN HOUSE
Solid paper: Chatterbox
Patterned paper: Chatterbox
Vellum: Provo Craft
Font: 2Peas Chestnuts
Nails: Chatterbox

JUNE & BABY TYLER
Patterned paper: Making
  Memories
Font: 2Peas Sailboat
Embroidery floss: DMC

Embellish with Patterned Paper

STELLA
Paper: Treehouse Memories
Vellum: Provo Craft
Font: 2Peas Tubby
Tag: Making Memories
Twill tape: May Arts
Safety pin: Robert's Crafts
Ribbon: Making Memories

EASTER EGG HUNT
Paper: Treehouse Memories
Vellum: Provo Craft
Font: 2Peas Chatter
Concho: Scrapworks

3-D HEART
Solid paper: Provo Craft
Patterned paper: Treehouse
  Memories
Vellum: Provo Craft
Font: Maiandra GD
Dotlets: Doodlebug
Ribbon: Making Memories
Fluid chalk ink: ColorBox

BRIAN
Solid paper: Bazzill Basics
Patterned paper: KI Memories
Vellum: Provo Craft
Font: Centaur
Rivets: Chatterbox

BRYNNE
Paper: Treehouse Memories
Vellum: Provo Craft
Fluid chalk ink: ColorBox
Font: 2Peas Tubby

GIFT II
Solid paper: Bazzill Basics
Patterned paper: American Crafts
Vellum: Provo Craft
Tag: unknown
Safety pin: Roberts Crafts
Flower accent: Jolee's Boutique
Fluid chalk ink: ColorBox
Font: 2Peas Sailboat
Twill tape: May Arts

STRAWBERRIES
Solid paper: Bazzill Basics
Patterned paper: Lasting
  Impressions
Vellum: Provo Craft
Font: Tw Cen MT
Eyelets: Doodlebug

SAILBOAT
Patterned paper: Sweetwater
Vellum: Provo Craft
Font: CK Toggle
Eyelets: Making Memories

PRESTON JAMES
Solid paper: Bazzill Basics
Patterned frame: My Mind's Eye
Font: Tw Cen MT
Eyelets: Making Memories
String: Unknown
Tag: Making Memories
Safety pin: Roberts Crafts

WELCOMING
Photograph: Hillary Black
Solid blue paper: Bazzill Basics
Solid white paper: Provo Craft
Patterned paper: Created on a
  computer
Font: 2Peas Highlight
Ribbon: All My Memories
Zipper pull: All My Memories

Embellish with Premade Artwork

FALL FEAST
Leaf die cuts: My Mind's Eye
Solid paper: Provo Craft
Patterned paper: Chatterbox
Vellum: Provo Craft
Font: Book Antiqua
Eyelets: Making Memories

BUZZ
Bee die cuts: My Mind's Eye
Solid paper: Bazzill Basics
Font: CK Plain Jane
Daisy brad: Provo Craft

BAILEY
Gift die cut: My Mind's Eye
Solid paper: Bazzill Basics
Patterned paper: KI Memories
Vellum: Provo Craft
Font: CK Handprint

DUCKLING
Duckling embellishment: Jolee's
  Boutique
Patterned paper: Making
  Memories
Font: 2Peas Tubby
Ribbon: Making Memories

THANKSGIVING FEAST
Turkey die cut: Embossible
  Designs
Solid paper: Provo Craft
Patterned paper: Chatterbox
Vellum: Provo Craft
Font: AL Handcrafted
Eyelets: Making Memories

HAPPY MOTHER'S DAY
Flower die cut: O' Scrap
Solid paper: Bazzill Basics
Vellum: Provo Craft
Font: 2Peas Tubby

BIRTHDAY GIRL
"Birthday Girl" die cut: Treehouse Memories
Solid paper: Treehouse Memories
Patterned paper: Treehouse Memories
Font: Impact

TEAM PARTY II
Baseball 3-D embellishments: Jolee's Boutique
Solid red paper: Bazzill Basics
"Leather" paper: Paper Adventures
Vellum: Provo Craft
Font: 2Peas Highlight
Eyelets: Making Memories

PANCAKE BREAKFAST
Star die cut: My Mind's Eye
Solid paper: Bazzill Basics
Patterned paper: Lasting Impressions
Vellum: Provo Craft
Font: CK Plain Jane
Brads: Provo Craft

BROOKLYN
Gift "token": Doodlebug
Patterned paper: Scrapworks
Vellum: Provo Craft
Font: 2Peas Highlight
Eyelets: Making Memories
Embroidery floss: DMC

Embellish with Photos

SIMON JAMES
Font: Tw Cen MT

CARTER LUCAS
Patterned paper: KI Memories
Vellum: Provo Craft
Font: Tw Cen MT
Tag: Making Memories

BETHANY JEAN COLLETTE
Patterned paper: Making Memories
Vellum: Provo Craft
Font: 2Peas Sailboat
Ribbon: Unknown

"80"
Patterned paper: Chatterbox
Vellum: Provo Craft
Font: AL Updated Classic
Nails: Chatterbox
Striped ribbon: May Arts
Velvet ribbon: Unknown
Embroidery Floss: DMC
"80" charms: unknown

CONNER RAY
Solid paper: Chatterbox
Vellum: Provo Craft
Font: 2Peas Sailboat
Snaps: Making Memories

CLAYTON DENNIS
Photograph: Julie Blodgett
Patterned paper: Making Memories
Vellum: Provo Craft
Font: 2Peas Chestnut
Ribbon: All My Memories
Charm: Marian & Me

MCKENZIE
Solid paper: Chatterbox
Patterned paper: Chatterbox
Vellum: Provo Craft
Font: CK Toggle

JOSH
Solid paper: Bazzill Basics
Vellum: Provo Craft
Font: AL Highlight
Eyelets, snaps, and photo anchors: Making Memories

KAMBREE NICOLE
Patterned paper: Making Memories
Vellum: Provo Craft
Fonts: Maiandra GD, AL Savannah
Eyelets: Making Memories
Ribbon: Making Memories

KENNA KAY
Solid paper: Provo Craft
Patterned paper: Making Memories
Font: AL Handcrafted

Embellish with Other Finds

PEBBLE
Pebble: Robert's Crafts
Solid paper: Provo Craft
Patterned paper: Chatterbox
Font: 2Peas Tasklist

JEWEL
Jewel: Unknown
Solid paper: Bazzill Basics
Patterned paper: Unknown
Vellum: Provo Craft
Font: CK Journaling

LEXI
Letter charms: Unknown
Solid paper: Bazzill Basics
Patterned paper: PSX
Font: CK Journaling
Eyelets: Making Memories
Ribbon: Offray
Foam squares: Therm O Web

PACIFIER
Pacifier: Unknown
Patterned paper: Making Memories
Vellum: Provo Craft
Font: Tw Cen MT
Eyelets: Doodlebug
Hemp: May Arts

DECORATIVE CLIP
Paper clip: Making Memories
Solid paper: Chatterbox
Patterned paper: KI Memories
Vellum: Provo Craft
Font: Myriad

DIAPER PIN
Diaper pin: Target
Beads: Jo-Ann Stores
Solid paper: Bazzill Basics
Patterned paper: Basic Grey
Vellum: Provo Craft
Font: Centaur

TAG
Solid paper: Provo Craft
Patterned paper: American Crafts
Vellum: Provo Craft
Font: 2Peas Renaissance
Stamps: Hero Arts
Mini clothespin: Unknown
Tag: Making Memories
Twill: May Arts
Embroidery floss: DMC

SILK FLOWER
Flower: Robert's Crafts
Patterned paper: Making Memories
Vellum: Provo Craft
Font: 2Peas Renaissance
Daisy Brad: Unknown

Embellish with an Enhanced Word

LOVE
Paper: Basic Grey
Vellum: Provo Craft
Font: AL Handcrafted
Embroidery floss: DMC
Ribbon: Unknown

LGC
Paper: Making Memories
Vellum: Provo Craft
Font: 2Peas Sailboat
Ribbon: May Arts

LUCY
Solid paper: Bazzill Basics
Patterned paper: KI Memories
Vellum: Provo Craft
Font: Tw Cen MT
Foam squares: Therm O Web

JACK
Solid paper: Provo Craft
Patterned paper: KI Memories
Vellum: Provo Craft
Font: Tw Cen MT
Eyelets: Making Memories
Hemp: May Arts

COME
Solid paper: Bazzill Basics
Patterned paper: KI Memories
Font: CK Journaling
Eyelets: Doodlebug
Embroidery floss: DMC

STAMPED JACK
Solid paper: Provo Craft
Patterned paper: S.E.I.
Font: Tw Cen MT
Alphabet stamps: Unknown

MAYA
Solid paper: Bazzill Basics
Patterned paper: Doodlebug
Font: Maiandra GD
Eyelets: Doodlebug

ALEXIS MAY
Solid paper: Provo Craft
Patterned Paper: S.E.I.
Vellum: Provo Craft
Fonts: Tw Cen MT, Lucida Calligraphy
Eyelets: Making Memories

Embellish with Buttons

BOOK CLUB
Solid paper: Provo Craft
Patterned paper: Chatterbox
Vellum: Provo Craft
Font: 2Peas Tubby
Button: Unknown

BUTTON WRAP
Solid paper: Provo Craft
Patterned paper: Scrapworks
Buttons: Making Memories
Embroidery floss: DMC

HANNAH JANE
Solid paper: Bazzill Basics
Patterned paper: S.E.I.
Vellum: Provo Craft
Font: CK Handprint
Button: Unknown

ANNALYSE HARTMAN
Solid paper: Making Memories
Patterned paper: Making Memories
Vellum: Provo Craft
Font: 2Peas Sailboat
Button: Making Memories
Embroidery floss: DMC

TYING THE KNOT
Patterned paper: Basic Grey
Vellum: Provo Craft
Font: AL Updated Classic
Hemp: May Arts
Fluid chalk ink: ColorBox

JAXON
Solid paper: Provo Craft
Patterned paper: Unknown
Font: Tw Cen MT
Button: Unknown
Embroidery thread: DMC

SAMANTHA CLARK
Solid paper: Provo Craft
Patterned paper: Chatterbox
Vellum: Provo Craft
Font: 2Peas Sailboat
Buttons: Unknown

HAPPY BIRTHDAY PAM
Solid paper: American Crafts
Patterned paper: American Crafts
Font: AL Handcrafted
Buttons: Unknown
Embroidery thread: DMC

Envelopes

BRIANA NEWTON
Envelope: Spectrum
Font: 2Peas Tasklist

ROBERT & LORENA
Solid paper: Provo Craft
Patterned paper: Treehouse Memories
Transparent envelope: American Crafts
Font: 2Peas Sailboat